REACH OUT FOR THE TREASURE

DR. CHUKWUNENYE ONUOHA

Foreword By Patrick McWhorter

Reach Out For The Treasure

Copyright © 2020 by Dr. Chukwunenye Onuoha

Cover design by Pastor Emeka Williams

Unless otherwise noted, scripture quotations are from the New King James Version of the Bible.

All rights are reserved. No part of this publication may be reproduced, stored in a retrieval system, or transmitted in any form or by any means – electronic, mechanical, photocopying, recording or otherwise – without the written permission of the author.

ISBN-13: 978-1-7336624-9-9

Printed in the United States of America

2020 – First Edition

Published by

6148 Jones Road, Flowery Branch, GA 30542

DEDICATION

This book is dedicated to all the frontline workers who risked their lives during the 2020 COVID 19 pandemic in USA and around the world.

May God bless them and grant them their hearts' desires.

ACKNOWLEDGMENT

I sincerely acknowledge and appreciate the leadership and guidance of the Holy Spirit in my life and in my ministry.

The Holy Spirit did not design the lockdown experience to become a knockdown. Rather He turned it around for me and inspired me to write two books; they are *Five Secrets Of Overcoming Fear*, and this pristine masterpiece, *Reach Out For The Treasure*.

PREFACE

In 2 Corinthians 4:7, the scripture says: *"But we have this treasure in earthen vessels, that the excellency of the power may be of God, and not of us."*

Words are not enough to describe the enormous treasures that can be revealed and discovered in the Kingdom of God. The Spirit of God in man hosts and preserves them in our lives.

People oftentimes don't know how gifted they are, and, through negligence, they sometimes lose what God has deposited in them.

In this book, the eight chapters have subtitles as follows:

1. WHEN IT IS FOUND

2. YOU ARE GIFTED

3. APPEARANCE AND REALITY

4. THE TREASURE

5. PAY THE PRICE

6. YOUR CHOICE

7. 3DS FOR TREASURE

8. DUTY CALL

These chapters will help you dream big, discover yourself, dwell in God's presence, and reach out for things with eternal value.

Your choice is your life and this book will prepare you to pay the price for the high calling of your destiny. You will also discover the purpose of God's gifts in your life, which is service to God's children and bringing glory to God.

You will also be challenged to develop your spiritual capacity for appropriation of divine deposits. Do not allow any good thing to elude you. Let God guide you and open your eyes to find treasures wherever they are, and to possess your possessions, securing your eternal destiny.

Contents

DEDICATION	5
ACKNOWLEDGMENT	7
PREFACE	9
INTRODUCTION	13
FOREWORD	17
Chapter 1 – WHEN IT IS FOUND	21
Chapter 2 – YOU ARE GIFTED	27
Chapter 3 – APPEARANCE AND REALITY	39
Chapter 4 – THE TREASURE	47
Chapter 5 – PAY THE PRICE	57
Chapter 6 – YOUR CHOICE	67
Chapter 7 – 3Ds FOR TREASURE	83
Chapter 8 – DUTY CALL	97
CONCLUSION	107

INTRODUCTION

Jesus told Peter to launch his vessel into the deep and lower his net for a great catch. Peter's reply was that they had toiled all night without catching any fish. However, he added, *"But at thy word, I will cast my net."*

His obedience got him and his friends a net-breaking school of fish. Jesus also told him to follow Him, and Peter abandoned everything to follow Jesus.

Now, I think that Peter launched even deeper when he decided to follow Jesus, and the Lord promised to make him a fisher of men.

Treasure is a concentration of wealth of any kind or form – something of great worth or value. Also, treasure is something concealed, hidden or buried from the ordinary senses of seeing, feeling or touching. It is something prepared, made ready, but not easily accessible without determination and tenacity.

Apart from physical treasures like money,

precious metals such as gold, silver etc., treasure includes strength, power, grace, mercy, kindness, love, peace, truth, life and all virtues of intrinsic values. Also, good health, humility, nobility, righteousness, integrity, honesty, character, and even YOU! These are great treasures.

Man is a great treasure! You are priceless! All treasures are owned and are given by the Lord God almighty. We can see this in James 1:17:

"Every good and every perfect gift is from above and cometh down from the Father of lights, with whom is no variableness, neither shadow of turning."

What more can we say? There is no treasure outside God. God is the source of every treasure. Seeking Him is seeking every treasure that leads to life fulfillment on planet earth.

Praise God!

Treasures are rarely on the surface. You must dig deep to get things with great value, in the same way you must dig deep to get coal, copper, gold, crude oil, etc.

In my home in Nigeria, you must dig over 600 feet into the ground for a well to reach clean water. It is also very expensive, as it could cost over four million naira (more than $10,000 USD) to complete. At the time of this publication, we have only one good well in my entire village.

When you go fishing, your fishing line must be long enough to go a certain depth, in order to catch the fish you want. Sometimes, they go to the bottom, and you may fish all day with your bait at a higher level without catching anything.

It is your choice where you want to lay down your net; whether on the surface or deep down in the depth of the sea.

Treasures don't come to you overnight. You have to make up your mind what you want. You have to also wait patiently for it. The search for this treasure is the crux of this book.

This book seeks to create in you awareness of your unique nature and to expose the hidden treasures God has deposited in you. It will educate and encourage you to reach for this treasure, through a detailed, step by step approach.

And what are the benefits? This book will reveal and enumerate them as you reach for the treasure that God has placed in you.

FOREWORD

At times in the history of God's people, men have thought the riches of God could be defined on a map or carried in a bag or wallet.

Even today, multitudes treat money as though it were of the greatest importance in this life. However, money is a temporal blessing from God, one that is certainly useful for this world, but that can only benefit our eternal lives as it is used to further the Kingdom of God and to bless others on behalf of our Lord.

I believe Dr. Chukwenenye Onuoha – Dr. Chuks – has given true focus to the greatest treasures God has placed before men.

Jesus said, "*Lay not up for yourselves treasures upon earth, where moth and rust doth corrupt, and where thieves break through and steal. But lay up for yourselves treasures in Heaven, where neither moth nor rust doth corrupt, and where thieves do not break through nor steal.*"

Jesus admonishes us to focus on eternal treasures. God has greater gifts than tangible ones to give His children. That is why Jesus, in Luke 16, refers to money as "that which is least," and points us to "true riches," as the substance to be desired.

What are the true riches Jesus spoke of?

I believe they are expressed by the phrase, "*the manifold grace of God*," the multi-faceted treasures God made available for us so that we may steward them for the benefit of the Kingdom and the household of God.

In this book, Dr. Chuks urges us to pursue the real treasure, just as Paul urged us in Colossians 3:1-3

"*If ye then be risen with Christ, seek those things which are above, where Christ sitteth on the right hand of God. Set your affection on things above, not on things on the earth. For ye are dead, and your life is hid with Christ in God.*"

Reach Out For The Treasure shows us that, as the body of Christ, we should treasure what God treasures, which means that we should highly value the lives of all people, the gifts God has made available to the followers of Jesus Christ, and the very life of Christ He has given us to live.

Our focus should be on the eternal things that God gives us and that He will use to build in us the character of Jesus Christ, who is our Example for living – if we will allow Him to do that.

Dr. Chuks reminds us, too, of the high trust God places in us when He invests His treasures in our "earthen vessels."

The great value of the treasures demands stewardship by greatly valued vessels.

And while God made you to contain and use His most valued treasure, YOU also are a great treasure to Him.

In his book, Dr. Chuks is heralding this very important truth from the heart of God, one in which God calls His people to turn our hearts toward those qualities that can make us "profitable" servants in the Kingdom of God, as well as genuine sons and daughters of the King.

Many thanks to you, Dr. Chuks, for this indispensable teaching, and for the privilege of allowing me to commend your readers to the tremendous value of this latest work of yours. It is a vital message for the body of Christ, and is sorely needed.

Patrick McWhorter,
Author of *Faith is a Three-Legged Stool*

CHAPTER ONE

WHEN IT IS FOUND

Oh! What a joy, what a celebration when a treasure is found!

All the time, money, energy, skill and materials spent in searching for it have, at that point, paid off. Our pain has turned into power; our scars have turned into stars. Our obstacles have turned into miracles. Our stumbling stones have turned into stepping stones.

When you find God, you have found eternal blessing.

It is abnormal for someone not to rejoice after finding a treasure. The joy cannot be hidden. One of the most outstanding outward expressions of someone who has found a treasure is unspeakable joy.

It is important to note that while you are looking for a treasure, it will seem like you are losing. The truth is that you cannot lose in God. You have everything to gain.

Come along, my friend; get on board this train.

When you celebrate your treasure, people could come asking you the secret of your success, and I know you will not hesitate to tell everyone that you know Somebody who turned your sorrow into joy, who healed you without hurting you. Somebody who took your pain away. Somebody who gave you what money cannot buy.

Many have presented an ugly fragmented picture of Christ and have scared so many to death. God did not send His Son to the world to condemn it: rather that, through Him, the world might be saved.

He is our Treasure, and we are His.

Treasures, when found, need to be preserved. Whatever deposit you have discovered that the Lord has blessed you with, you must preserve. You cannot let it slip away from you.

Hold fast to your fate. Do not allow anything to steal your treasure away. The enemy will always want to steal from you what God has deposited in and with you. The enemy wants you to make light of divine deposits in you. Resist him and he will flee from you.

It is your duty to watch over whatever you treasure. You cannot be careless or complacent about it.

When a treasure is found, it is announced. If you buy an expensive trumpet and no one blows it, there will be no sound or music. God does not enter into a city without announcing Himself. When God deposits His treasure in you, He announces you and commands you to go and tell everybody.

We are witnesses to the manifold blessings of God. If you find peace in God, tell others. If you receive healing from the Lord, testify. It is for the glory of God that we announce His Kingdom on the earth. We are overcomers by the blood of the Lamb and the words of our testimonies.

When you find the treasure, remember to give all the glory to God. No man on earth should give glory to himself.

Humbling yourself before God is an act of glorifying God.

Every good and perfect gift is from above.

There are so many people before you that sought for what you have found, but they could not find it. It is not by your power, nor by your might, but is by the Spirit of the Lord.

When you glorify God for what He has given you, He will give you even more. Learn how to give God praise for the smallest thing you receive from Him.

Praise God in the morning, praise Him in the noon day and praise Him even when the sun goes down.

Learn how to celebrate the goodness of God always in your life. Rejoice evermore!

When you celebrate whatever God has blessed you with, you are asking God for more. To him that much is given, more will be given to him, and to him that is ungrateful, what he has will be taken away from him.

God will not tolerate anything standing in the way of people praising Him. The scripture declares that God inhabits the praises from His children. God does not want His glory to be shared with any other god: "*For thou shall worship no other god, for the Lord whose name is jealous, is a jealous God.*" (Exodus 34:14)

So many people don't celebrate what God has given them because it looks small in their eyes. The value you attach to what you have is the value of it. What you don't value may be a treasure to another.

Be careful when people tell you that what you have is nothing, because it might become something when it gets into their hands. Some people might be jealous over what you have. Do not worry about them because God cannot stop blessing you. In fact, some people being jealous of you is a sign that something good is coming to you.

When you find your treasure, you might be facing three categories of enemies. First, those who are envious; they are not happy that something good is happening to you.

Second are those who are jealous; they want to destroy what you have.

And third are those who want you dead because you are so blessed.

The first two categories are nothing to worry so much about, but the third category is very serious.

The good news is that God will always deliver you.

Remember, God can bless you with abundant blessings, but won't tell you what to do with them. You can use your gifts, talents, skills, your money, houses and lands the way you wish, but God will always come back to see what you – as His steward over them – have done with the blessings.

A day of judgment is coming when everyone will stand before God to give an account of how they used what He has given to them.

Whatever you are demanding from God right now, make sure your motives are right and your priorities are also right. When God sees your faithful heart, He will give you treasures in abundance.

CHAPTER TWO

YOU ARE GIFTED

You are gifted; please do not squander your gifts through negligence and ignorance!

God gives to everyone according to each person's ability. You are the best of God at any level of ability you have, and God cannot give you what you cannot handle.

The book of Ephesians 4:7 illustrates this clearly:

"But unto everyone of us is given grace according to the measure of the gift of Christ."

As you can see, everyone has got something from God. No one is empty. You can do something great because God has deposited a great treasure in you! Child of God, get ready! The treasure in you will manifest!

Praise God!

God expects us to treasure whatever He gives to us.

I do not want you to miss that last statement. Let me repeat it and expand upon it.

God expects us to treasure whatever He gives to us. He greatly desires for us to value His gifts the same way He does.

We need to put to work the various gifts God has given to us. I have never heard or read that God punished someone for doing too much good. However, one can be punished for doing nothing.

The parable of the talents is as good an illustration of that truth as can be seen; it is in Matthew 25:14-30:

"For the Kingdom of Heaven is as a man travelling into a far country, who called his own servants, and delivered unto them his goods. And unto one he gave five talents, to another two, and to another one; to every man according to his several ability; and straightway took his journey. Then he that had received the five talents went and traded with the same, and made them other five talents. And likewise he that had received

two, he also gained other two. But he that had received one went and digged in the earth, and hid his lord's money. After a long time the lord of those servants cometh, and reckoneth with them. And so he that had received five talents came and brought other five talents, saying, Lord, thou deliveredst unto me five talents: behold, I have gained beside them five talents more. His lord said unto him, Well done, thou good and faithful servant: thou hast been faithful over a few things, I will make thee ruler over many things: enter thou into the joy of thy lord. He also that had received two talents came and said, Lord, thou deliveredst unto me two talents: behold, I have gained two other talents beside them. His lord said unto him, Well done, good and faithful servant; thou hast been faithful over a few things, I will make thee ruler over many things: enter thou into the joy of thy lord. Then he which had received the one talent came and said, Lord, I knew thee that thou art an hard man, reaping where thou hast not sown, and gathering where thou hast not strawed: And I was afraid, and went and hid thy talent in the earth: lo, there thou hast that is thine. His lord answered and said unto him, Thou wicked and slothful servant, thou knewest that I reap where I sowed not, and gather where I have not strawed: Thou oughtest therefore to have put my money to the exchangers, and then at my coming I should have received mine own with usury. Take therefore the talent from him, and give it unto him which hath ten talents. For unto every one that hath shall be given, and he shall have abundance: but from him that hath not shall be taken away even that which he hath. And cast ye the unprofitable servant into outer darkness: there shall be weeping and gnashing of teeth."

As we have seen in the scripture above, the more you use what God has given you, He gives you even more.

You don't wait until things get better; rather you do the work that will *make* things better. It is not how hard you fight; it is all about what you are fighting for.

I charge you to discipline and persuade yourself to find what makes you special (that is your gift) and use it for God's glory and for the blessings of His children. I speak to you today; your gift will lift you!

As I said earlier, everyone has a special gift from God. You don't have to hide it. Your gift makes you unique and exceptional. It should be a blessing to you and to the Church of Jesus Christ. You must employ it for His service. The book of 1 Peter explains it clearly:

"As every man hath received the gift, even so minister the same one to another as good stewards of the manifold grace of God." (4:10)

No gift from God is too big and none is too small. Every gift is tailored to meet a specific need in the house of God, that the name of the Lord might be glorified. The same Lord is Lord over all; the same source - one God and one Spirit. The scripture in 1 Corinthians 12:4-12, explains it better:

"Now there are diversities of gifts, but the same Spirit. And there are differences of administrations, but the same Lord. And there are diversities of operations, but it is the same God which worketh all in all. But the manifestation of the Spirit is given to every man to profit withal. For to one is given by the Spirit the word of wisdom; to another the word of knowledge by the same Spirit; to another faith by the same Spirit; to another the gifts of healing by the same Spirit; to

another the working of miracles; to another prophecy; to another discerning of spirits; to another divers kinds of tongues; to another the interpretation of tongues: But all these worketh that one and the selfsame Spirit, dividing to every man severally as he will. For as the body is one, and hath many members, and all the members of that one body, being many, are one body: so also is Christ."

All gifts are meant to complement each other so that there is no need for competition in the house of God. *"...but they measuring themselves by themselves, and comparing themselves among themselves, are not wise"* as is stated in the book of 2 Corinthians (10:12).

You gift is your treasure! It will announce you! Hallelujah!

Listen to me, Child of God. DO NOT NEGLECT YOUR GIFT!

You must understand that whatever gift of God you neglect, you will certainly regret at last. Do not waste God's resources and yours. Developing your gift guarantees your fulfillment in life. Submit yourself to coaches and mentors - those that will teach and help you maximize God's deposits in you. Ask questions; don't be afraid to try. Don't be afraid to fail. Failure is part of the learning process and not your destination.

Above all, humble yourself and learn from the Holy Spirit. Let Him lead and guide. You will never be a waste! Any power assigned to waste your destiny is destroyed in Jesus' mighty name!

Praise God!

Samson was anointed from his mother's womb. God gave him a supernatural power in order to deliver the children of Israel from the hands of the Philistines. He squandered it through negligence. He was using selfishly the power God gave to him. He had to pay dearly for it.

The book of Judges, 16:1-30, tells us more:

"Then went Samson to Gaza, and saw there an harlot, and went in unto her. And it was told the Gazites, saying, Samson is come hither. And they compassed him in, and laid wait for him all night in the gate of the city, and were quiet all the night, saying, In the morning, when it is day, we shall kill him.

And Samson lay till midnight, and arose at midnight, and took the doors of the gate of the city, and the two posts, and went away with them, bar and all, and put them upon his shoulders, and carried them up to the top of an hill that is before Hebron. And it came to pass afterward, that he loved a woman in the valley of Sorek, whose name was Delilah. And the lords of the Philistines came up unto her, and said unto her, Entice him, and see wherein his great strength lieth, and by what means we may prevail against him, that we may bind him to afflict him; and we will give thee every one of us eleven hundred pieces of silver. And Delilah said to Samson, Tell me, I pray thee, wherein thy great strength lieth, and wherewith thou mightest be bound to afflict thee. And Samson said unto her, If they bind me with seven green withes that were never dried, then shall I be weak, and be as another man. Then the lords of the Philistines brought up to her seven green withes which had not been dried, and she bound him with them. Now there were men lying in wait, abiding with her in the chamber. And she said unto him, The Philistines be upon thee, Samson. And he brake the withes, as a thread of tow is broken when it toucheth the fire. So his strength was not known. And Delilah said unto Samson,

Behold, thou hast mocked me, and told me lies: now tell me, I pray thee, wherewith thou mightest be bound. And he said unto her, If they bind me fast with new ropes that never were occupied, then shall I be weak, and be as another man. Delilah therefore took new ropes, and bound him therewith, and said unto him, The Philistines be upon thee, Samson. And there were liers in wait abiding in the chamber. And he brake them from off his arms like a thread. And Delilah said unto Samson, Hitherto thou hast mocked me, and told me lies: tell me wherewith thou mightest be bound. And he said unto her, If thou weavest the seven locks of my head with the web. And she fastened it with the pin, and said unto him, The Philistines be upon thee, Samson. And he awaked out of his sleep, and went away with the pin of the beam, and with the web. And she said unto him, How canst thou say, I love thee, when thine heart is not with me? thou hast mocked me these three times, and hast not told me wherein thy great strength lieth. And it came to pass, when she pressed him daily with her words, and urged him, so that his soul was vexed unto death; That he told her all his heart, and said unto her, There hath not come a razor upon mine head; for I have been a Nazarite unto God from my mother's womb: if I be shaven, then my strength will go from me, and I shall become weak, and be like any other man. And when Delilah saw that he had told her all his heart, she sent and called for the lords of the Philistines, saying, Come up this once, for he hath showed me all his heart. Then the lords of the Philistines came up unto her, and brought money in their hand. And she made him sleep upon her knees; and she called for a man, and she caused him to shave off the seven locks of his head; and she began to afflict him, and his strength went from him. And she said, The Philistines be upon thee, Samson. And he awoke out of his sleep, and said, I will go out as at other times before, and shake myself. And he wist not that the LORD was departed from him. But the Philistines took him, and put out his eyes, and brought him down to Gaza, and bound him with fetters of brass; and he did grind in the prison house. Howbeit the hair of his head began to grow again after he was shaven. Then the lords of the Philistines gathered them together for to offer a great sacrifice unto Dagon their god, and to rejoice: for they said, Our god hath delivered Samson our enemy into our hand. And when the people saw him, they praised their god: for they said, Our god hath delivered into our hands our enemy, and the destroyer of our country, which slew many of us. And it came to pass, when their hearts were merry, that they said, Call for Samson, that he may make us sport. And they called for Samson out of the prison house; and he made them sport: and they set him between the pillars. And Samson said unto the lad that held him by the hand, Suffer me that I may feel the pillars whereupon the house standeth, that I may lean upon them. Now the house was full of men and women; and all the lords of the Philistines were there; and there were upon the roof about three thousand men and women, that beheld while Samson made sport. And Samson called unto the LORD, and said, O Lord God, remember me, I pray thee, and strengthen me, I pray thee, only this once, O God, that I may be at once avenged of the Philistines for my two eyes. And Samson took hold of the two middle pillars upon which the house stood, and on which it was borne up, of the one with his right hand, and of the other with his left. And Samson said, Let me die with the Philistines. And he bowed himself with all his might; and the house fell upon the lords, and upon all the people that were therein. So the dead which he slew at his death were more than they which he slew in his life."

From this scripture, we see that Samson was careless with the anointing of God in His life. He lacked character.

He was supposed to judge Israel for a long time. But his reign was cut short because he could not maintain God's statutes and ordinances upon his life.

Many believers today are like Samson, anointed, but without character. They are struggling with negative habits, urges and desires that move them to do things against their will or things they always regret afterwards, just like Samson, Judas Iscariot, and Gehazi, to mention but a few.

If you are such a one, reading this book, I pray for you today. Let every habit, hunger and evil urge that is limiting the manifestation of God in your life and ministry be destroyed!

Praise God!

You are unstoppable!

CHAPTER THREE

APPEARANCE AND REALITY

You don't measure the value of things just by the way they appear.

People are often deceived by the physical appearance of things, objects, people and places.

Today, we live in a world where most things you see with your natural eyes are not what they appear to be. Appearance is very different from reality.

Many people have made terrible mistakes in life due to lack of spiritual insight. Apostle Paul admonishes us on this truth in 2 Corinthians 4:18:

"While we look not at the things which are seen but at the things which are not seen: for the things which are seen are temporal; but the things which are not seen are eternal."

The unseen is more important than the seen.

Always check for the unseen realities. You need spiritual sensitivity and discernment as a child of God.

When Jesus saw Nathanael coming, in John 1:47, He said to him; *"Behold an Israelite indeed, in whom is no guile."*

Because this was their first meeting, Nathanael was so surprised that Jesus could talk about his personality without having had any interaction with him. His physical appearance had nothing to do with Jesus' assertion, for God observes the heart.

Child of God, stop looking at the outward appearance of people and things. Do not measure the value of things just by the way they appear.

One day I saw a beautiful girl and everyone around wanted to talk to her. I walked up to her and began to preach the gospel to her. I don't hesitate sharing my testimony of how Jesus saved me.

When she realized that I was a Christian, she asked me to pray for her because she was battling with breast cancer.

You see, she was very beautiful looking on the outside, but inside, she had breast cancer.

Be careful what you are reaching out for. Reach out for treasure not pleasure.

Praise God!

Gold, in its original form, might not look like gold at all.

It is a treasure, even though it has to pass through the fire. Crude oil might not mean anything to you when you look at it, ordinarily.

Do not judge anything by physical appearance only. Sometimes, it is not the quantity of a thing that matters; rather, it is the quality.

Great gifts sometimes come in small packages.

When I migrated to America in 2006, my cousin, Amara, gave me a gift of a used Honda Civic. On the outside, the car didn't look that wonderful, but on the inside, Amara had spent so much that the engine was as good as a brand new car.

When I received the car, someone (name withheld) mocked the car based on how the car looked outwardly. Her very words to me were, "Come and move your brand new car."

To the glory of God, this car served me for four years without going to the mechanic for any repairs whatsoever, either for engine or body repairs. This car was a treasure to me, and I am always grateful to God for touching my cousin to give me such a much needed gift at that time.

The hand of God was on this car throughout the period I used it. I experienced two incredible miracles while using this car.

One day, I came back from work with no money in my pocket and my gas tank was empty. I went to bed not knowing what to do in the morning. I just prayed my normal prayers and slept. In the morning, I went outside and observed that my gas tank cover area was wet. I could not figure out why. It did not rain in the night, and a closer look at it showed that it was not water on the car, but gas.

Coming from Nigeria, I thought maybe someone tried to drain gas from my car.

While I was wondering what must have happened, I had a leading to start the engine. To my greatest surprise, my fuel gauge read full.

I was speechless and in awe of God. This kind of miracle is hard to explain.

God filled my car with gas.

Secondly, remember that I told you I never did any repairs on this car throughout the four years I used it.

There was a day this car was pushed to the mechanic shop because it wouldn't start. The mechanic was so busy that he couldn't attend to my car. The next day I went to his shop and asked him to give me my car keys.

He said he was sorry he didn't have time to attend to my car yet. I insisted on getting my keys, and when he gave them to me, I got in my car by faith, and started it. The engine responded, and I drove off.

The car was never taken to a mechanic shop until I sold the car to upgrade to a bigger car. You see, the outward appearance of this car might have been deceitful, but it was a treasure for me.

Sister Amara, thank you so much for the gift!

Let us consider what the Bible said in 1 Samuel 16:4-13:

"And Samuel did that which the LORD spake, and came to Bethlehem. And the elders of the town trembled at his coming, and said, Comest thou peaceably? And he said, Peaceably: I am come to sacrifice unto the LORD: sanctify yourselves, and come with me to the sacrifice. And he sanctified Jesse and his sons, and called them to the sacrifice. And it came to pass, when they were come, that he looked on Eliab, and said, Surely the LORD's anointed is before him. But the LORD said unto Samuel, Look not on his countenance, or on the height of his stature; because I have refused him: for the LORD seeth not as man seeth; for man looketh on the outward appearance, but the LORD looketh on the heart. Then Jesse called Abinadab, and made him pass before Samuel. And he said, Neither hath the LORD chosen this. Then Jesse made Shammah to pass by. And he said, Neither hath the LORD chosen this. Again, Jesse made seven of his sons to pass before Samuel. And Samuel said unto Jesse, The LORD hath not chosen these. And Samuel said unto Jesse, Are

here all thy children? And he said, There remaineth yet the youngest, and, behold, he keepeth the sheep. And Samuel said unto Jesse, Send and fetch him: for we will not sit down till he come hither. And he sent, and brought him in. Now he was ruddy, and withal of a beautiful countenance, and goodly to look to. And the LORD said, Arise, anoint him: for this is he. Then Samuel took the horn of oil, and anointed him in the midst of his brethren: and the Spirit of the LORD came upon David from that day forward. So Samuel rose up, and went to Ramah."

David was a treasure in the house of his father, Jesse. God wanted a king that would replace Saul.

According to the scriptures above, when Samuel saw the older sons of Jesse and thought they were the chosen of the Lord, God said no, *"Look not on his countenance, or on the height of his stature; because I have refused him: for the LORD seeth not as man seeth; for man looketh on the outward appearance, but the LORD looketh on the heart"*

Samuel was looking at the outward appearance of the sons of Jesse, but God was looking at the heart.

Jesse, on the other hand, never expected that David, the small boy he kept in the bush to tend his sheep, would be the chosen.

As I said before, "great gifts sometimes come in small packages!"

My prayer for you is that, henceforth, you will start seeing things the way God sees them, in Jesus' mighty name!

Hallelujah!

CHAPTER FOUR

THE TREASURE

One thing you need to know as a child of God is that you are unique in your own way.

You are beautiful, and handsome, because God, the almighty Creator, has made you so.

God has created you to be priceless, smart and wise. All you need to do is to develop the consciousness that you are special because God made you in His very own image.

Every time you look in the mirror, say to yourself that you are the image of God. It does not matter whether your face is beautiful or your head is genius, you are the image of God, and that is all that matters.

What people say about you should not be a factor in your life at all. What matters most is what God says about you.

Let us consider the following scriptures:

"I will praise thee; for I am fearfully and wonderfully made: marvellous are thy works; and that my soul knoweth right well." Psalm 139:14

"But ye are a chosen generation, a royal priesthood, an holy nation, a peculiar people; that ye should shew forth the praises of him who hath called you out of darkness into his marvellous light." 1 Peter 2:9

"For the LORD's portion is his people; Jacob is the lot of his inheritance. He found him in a desert land, and in the waste howling wilderness; he led him about, he instructed him, he kept him as the apple of his eye." Deuteronomy 32:9-10

"For thus saith the LORD of hosts; after the glory hath he sent me unto the nations which spoiled you: for he that toucheth you toucheth the apple of his eye." Zechariah 2:8

You are precious to God! He has deposited something in you that made you priceless. No amount of money can equal your value, because of what God has deposited in you. The scriptures above said it all. You are not just wonderfully made. You are the apple of God's eyes. You are the chosen generation and the Lord's portion.

Child of God, you are the best.

Listen to me: you need to understand this truth so that you can reach for treasures that God has deposited in and around you.

You may not look like it now, but listen to the word of God, believe and live by it. You are what the Word of God says you are!

Let's take a look at the scripture in the book of 2 Corinthians. It says, *"But we have this treasure in earthen vessels, that the excellency of the power will be of God and not of us."* (4:7)

Here, Paul the apostle was not just talking to some people. Rather, he was talking to *all believers*, including you and me. He said that we have this priceless, precious, unique, expensive and high quality item in an earthen vessel.

In the Jewish tradition, they have this earthen vessel designed as a "potty," which people use to pee in, and it's kept outside. It is smelly and stinky because of what it is used for.

But what if you are informed that someone just dropped a million-dollar diamond inside the potty? Then, if you are asked to pick it up, you just bend, squeeze your face, cover your nose with one hand, and use the other to bring out the diamond. Right?

Child of God, that is exactly what God has done for you and me. Even though, without Him, we might have been a bit stinky, He decided to deposit something precious and priceless in us as His children.

He did something in your life that makes you priceless.

Praise God. You just need to understand this!

For those of you who are married, for example, I want you to understand that your spouse has something in him/her that is priceless, and that is what attracted you to him/her in the first place.

Even if you are not seeing that thing now, I want you to know that the very point of attraction is still there in your spouse. God deposited it in the first place.

There is something that God has deposited in your life which the enemy can never take away.

People easily give up on themselves, their families, spouses, and friends because they think that something is missing.

Believe me, nothing changed in your spouse. As a matter of fact, you were the one that changed.

You no longer appreciate your spouse; you do not express your love to your spouse anymore. You used to give attention to your spouse, listen to him/her, among other things. But you no longer do these things. Yet you complain that your spouse has changed a lot.

No, he/she has not changed. Just look within. If you set aside quality time to spend with your spouse, he/she will always want to come home to you as soon as possible.

Your spouse will not have any games to play when you make him/her comfortable.

We all have these treasures packaged in

earthen vessels. **All you need to do is to reach out for the treasure and not the earthen vessel**. It is what God has deposited in our lives that counts.

I know that, as a child of God, you hate hell, so do not make your home to be like hell.

You love Heaven, so demonstrate Heaven in your home.

You know that when you want to buy a new car or some other item, sometimes you are given a "demo" for you to get familiar with the item. In the same vein, I implore you to "demo" Heaven in your home here on earth, because before the "sweet bye and bye," there is the "sweet now and now."

I want us to look at the scripture, 2 Corinthians 4:7, more carefully. I need you to know that the *"earthen vessel"* Paul was talking about is you and the *"treasure"* refers to that unique and priceless virtue which God has embedded inside you: *that* is your ***ministry***. And the phrase, *"**the excellency of power**"* means that God is going to work something out with the treasure He has deposited in you, and everything is going to be to His glory.

Hallelujah!

In verse 1 of 2 Corinthians 4, the Bible says; "***Therefore seeing we have this ministry as we have received mercy, we faint not.***"

We received the ministry, and we know it is the mercy of God that gave it to us and not our works of righteousness, nor anything that we have done - or even what we *will* do.

Rather, we got it because of what God has done by giving us His Son Jesus Christ. For "*we have been saved by grace, and not by works, lest any man should boast.*" (Ephesians 2:8-9).

It is the gift of God. We have received this ministry which comes as mercy to us. And because it is God that has shown us this mercy, we do not lose heart.

I want you to understand that the ministry God has given to you is not just for keeps, meaning, not just for your benefit, but it is for you to minister unto others. We have become selfish and self-centered, in that we neglect to serve others through the ministry (treasures) God has given to us.

God is deliberately keeping you on earth for

you to expand His Kingdom and reduce the kingdom of darkness, and to serve Him effectively with the ministry He has given to you. Your ministry is for you to serve.

I want to make an illustration with two water bottles, one filled to the brim and the other empty.

As Christians, our lives are like the bottles. The filled water bottle exemplifies a "Spirit-filled" child of God, while the empty one represents a child of God without the Holy Spirit.

When your life is empty, the enemy can come in at any time. And when the devil creeps into any life, he never shows any iota of mercy. He sets to work immediately; he begins to squeeze the person, and he goes on and on. He pays no attention to the cries of woe that emanate from the life he is squeezing.

The scripture says that "*the thief cometh not but steal, to kill and to destroy*," but Jesus has come "*that we might have life and have it more abundantly*." (John 10:10)

Hallelujah!

Your treasure (gift) is your ministry, which you have received by mercy for the service of the saints!

Reach out for the treasure now, in Jesus' mighty name!

CHAPTER FIVE

PAY THE PRICE

I'm sure you have heard the popular saying, "There is no free lunch."

I completely agree, because there is always a catch for the supposed free lunch. The "free lunch" is usually either NOT free, or NOT EVEN CLOSE to a lunch that someone would actually want to consume.

When we look at things of great value, the saying is even more pertinent. It must cost you something to acquire things of great value.

To get what you treasure, you should be ready to pay the price.

Treasures are not cheap.

In Luke 14:28, Jesus asked a question: *"Which of you intending to build a tower sitteth not down first and counteth the cost, whether he has sufficient to finish it?"*

It is not enough just to start when you go about acquiring treasure; you must be determined to finish, and finish well.

Therefore, you have to make preparations to pay the price in order to finish every step you are taking to reach out for the treasure you seek.

Praise God!

In John 12:3, the Bible says, *"Then took Mary a pound of ointment of spikenard very costly and anointed the feet of Jesus and wiped his feet with her hair and the house was filled with the odor of the ointment."*

When you find a rare or valuable product you are diligently looking for, cost does not matter anymore. Mary had to break a pound jar of ointment of spikenard that was very expensive, and when she did, she got what the ointment could not give her.

She paid the price and became part and parcel of the gospel message. She was privileged to be the first to see Jesus when He rose from the dead - an honor that

Apostle Peter, the leader of the apostles, did not receive.

Consider that Mary spared no expense, giving up a precious possession for the Lord's glory.

I challenge you today to pay the price.

You've got all it takes!

Praise God!

Also consider David.

When the prophet told David to raise up an altar unto the LORD in a certain place - on the site of the threshing floor of Araunah the Jebusite – he went immediately to obey. The problem was, David did not own that threshing floor.

When he approached Araunah to buy the threshing floor, the man offered to give it to King David.

But listen to how David answered him.

David said, *"Neither will I offer burnt offering unto the Lord my God of that which doth cost me nothing*" (2 Samuel 24:24).

There is nothing you do for the sake of God's Kingdom that is too much. No offering, devotion, dedication, nor any commitment is too much. No prayer or fasting is too much.

Remember that it is God that has given you the power to do that which is pleasing in His sight.

A lot of people give excuses and allow laziness to ruin their destiny. Procrastination is a lazy man's slogan. God has given us all that pertains to life and godliness: 2 Peter 1:3.

There is no room for excuses.

There is no need to do defer for tomorrow what ought be done now.

Having done all to stand, STAND NOW!

Pay the price!

Hallelujah!

The Bible says in Philippians 3:14, *"I press toward the mark for the prize of the high calling of God in Christ Jesus."*

The apostle Paul made very clear the approach he took towards reaching his treasure. He said "*I press.*"

This shows that he did not pay the price out of convenience. He paid the price in chains and in prison, but he made it.

Child of God, you will make it!

Take your place! Stand your ground! Pay the price! Victory is yours!

Praise God!

Unlike Mary, your own price may not be something that money will buy. It might be humility, obedience, suffering unjustly as Joseph did, or fourteen years of service, the way Jacob worked for his treasure.

Consider the Gethsemane experience of the Lord Jesus. Whatever may be required of you, as a child of God, you have all it takes.

God will not put on you more than you can bear. No matter the trials that you encounter, with the help of the Spirit of God, you will come out victorious.

No wonder the scripture says in

2 Corinthians 4:8-9:

"We are troubled on every side, yet not distressed; we are perplexed, but not in despair; persecuted, but not forsaken; cast down, but not destroyed."

Also in Romans 8:35-39, Apostle Paul made a profound statement about the power of God to overcome every trial:

"Who shall separate us from the love of Christ? Shall tribulation, or distress, or persecution, or famine, or nakedness, or peril, or sword? As it is written, For thy sake we are killed all the day long; we are accounted as sheep for the slaughter. Nay, in all these things we are more than conquerors through him that loved us. For I am persuaded, that neither death, nor life, nor angels, nor principalities, nor powers, nor things present, nor things to come, nor height, nor depth, nor any other creature, shall be able to separate us from the love of God, which is in Christ Jesus our Lord."

Therefore, as a child of God that is filled with the Spirit of God, you just need to know that what you go through does not impact negatively on the treasure that God has deposited in you.

So no matter how the devil presses and squeezes you, you will still come out stronger because of the treasure inside of you, and nothing will be able to separate you from the love of God in Christ Jesus.

Praise God!

In another scripture, the Bible encourages us to understand that every affliction ends in glory. It reads:

"For our light affliction which is but for a moment, worketh for us a far more exceeding and eternal weight of glory."

All we need is to fix our attention on Jesus, the Author and Finisher of our faith. (Hebrews 12:2)

For we know that all things are working for our good because we love the Lord and are the called according to His purpose. (Romans 8:28)

Hallelujah!

Romans 8:18 assures us further that, whatever sufferings or trials we pass through now can never be compared to the glory that will be revealed in us!

I pray for you, child of God; may you receive all it takes to pay the price for the glory of God to be revealed in your life!

God sees us as His only treasure on planet earth. God loves us so much that he cannot allow us to perish. We carry His DNA.

When the first Adam failed, God lost every one of us. It cost God His only begotten Son to be able to buy us back.

Love is expensive.

Greater love has no man than this. Jesus paid the ultimate price to win us back. If God did not spare His Son because of you, what, then, are we hiding from Him?

There was this story of a man that was hospitalized and he spent months and months in a ventilator. When he recovered, he was given a bill of half a million dollars. When he opened the bill, he started crying, and everyone thought it was because of the high hospital bill.

The doctor walked up to him and said, "I

know that the bill we gave you is too high; I can reduce it for you."

The man cried even more, and said to the doctor, "I am a multi-millionaire. Your bill is not a problem at all. I can take care of it right now. I am crying because I have been breathing God's air all these years without a bill."

Heaven is the greatest treasure to reach out for. No cost is too much to inherit God's Kingdom!

CHAPTER SIX

YOUR CHOICE

Let us start this chapter with Deuteronomy 30:19:

"I call Heaven and earth to record this day against you, that I have set before you life and death, blessing and cursing: therefore choose life, that both thou and thy seed may live."

Life is all about choices.

Our present circumstances are products of the choices we made yesterday. That is why it is very important for you to pay attention to the choices you are making today; they definitely define your tomorrow.

The treasures you are reaching out for today will determine your crown tomorrow. Moses refused to be called the son of Pharaoh's daughter, but, instead, chose to suffer affliction with God's people, as it's recorded in Hebrews 11:24:

"By faith Moses, when he was come to years, refused to be called the son of Pharaoh's daughter, choosing rather to suffer affliction with the people of God, than to enjoy the pleasures of Egypt; esteeming the reproach of Christ greater than the treasures of Egypt: for he had respect unto the recompense of the reward."

Here, Moses had a choice to make: becoming the grandson of Pharaoh, the greatest and most powerful man on planet earth then; it was a position of royalty, one that many people would have jumped at and maintained at any cost.

But he made a choice that gave him the opportunity to talk to God face to face. You and I would not know and read about Moses today if he hadn't made the right choice, to identify with God.

On the other hand, Lot chose to go and live in the plain of Jordan, which is Sodom and Gomorrah. He looked and saw that the land was well watered, so he made his choice. He was almost destroyed – and would have been, if not for Abraham, the friend of God.

Not only that, but Lot's wife became a pillar of salt; his daughters lured him to commit incest with them, which gave birth to the cursed nations of Moab and Ammon. (Genesis 13:10; Genesis 19:30-38)

All these are the consequences of making wrong choice or reaching out for wrong treasures. A lot of destinies have been destroyed because of this.

But listen to me, child of God. You will not make the wrong choices! You will not be deceived by the vanities of this world! The Holy Spirit will help you to make right choices and to reach out for God's ordained treasures, for your calling and destiny, in Jesus' mighty name!

Praise God!

Let us also consider the story of Elijah and Elisha.

We will look at how Elisha chose to reach out for the treasure in the life of his master, how he paid the price despite all distractions.

We will also compare this to the life of Gehazi, the servant of Elisha, and see how the latter sold out his destiny cheaply for worldly treasures.

It's your choice. Determine your price and your price determines the value (treasure) you will receive.

I pray for you today that you will make the right choice henceforth, and will reach out for the treasures God has deposited and ordained for your life and destiny!

Hallelujah!

Elisha served Elijah for twenty years without a paycheck. When it was time for God to take Elijah home, Elijah gave Elisha a lifetime opportunity to ask for whatever he wanted. He chose to reach out for the treasure that was in the life of Elijah by asking for the double portion of the spirit of Elijah.

Elijah told him that he had asked for a difficult thing. However, he told Elisha that if he saw him being taken up, it would be done for him.

It should be noted that Elijah was mightily used by God in his days. God used Elijah to perform eight outstanding miracles. Let's look at those:

EIGHT MIRACLES OF ELIJAH

1. Elijah commanded the heavens not to rain for a period of three and half years in Israel during the reign of King Ahab. And it did not rain for three and half years, according to the word of Elijah.

"Elias was a man subject to like passions as we are, and he prayed earnestly that it might not rain: and it rained not on the earth by the space of three years and six months. And he prayed again, and the heaven gave rain, and the earth brought forth her fruit." (James 5:17-18)

Also read 1 Kings 17:1.

2. Ravens brought Elijah bread and fish every day while he was in hiding far away from his home. Only God knew where he was, and the birds never missed finding his address. (1 Kings 17:6)

"And the ravens brought him bread and flesh in the morning, and bread and flesh in the evening; and he drank of the brook."

3. God instructed a poor widow of Zarephath to feed Elijah, and when she did, her barrel of meal and her cruse of oil did not dry up. (1 Kings 17:16)

"And the barrel of meal wasted not, neither did the cruse of oil fail, according to the word of the LORD, which he spake by Elijah."

4. Elijah raised the dead son of the widow back to life. (1 Kings17:22)

"And the LORD heard the voice of Elijah; and the soul of the child came into him again, and he revived."

5. Fire fell from Heaven on Mount Carmel and burned the wood, licked the waters and consumed the sacrifice. (1 Kings 18:38)

"Then the fire of the LORD fell, and consumed the burnt sacrifice, and the wood, and the stones, and the dust, and licked up the water that was in the trench."

6. Elijah called down fire to consume King Ahaziah's captain and his fifty men assigned to arrest Elijah. (2 Kings 1:10)

"And Elijah answered and said to the captain of fifty, If I be a man of God, then let fire come down from Heaven, and consume thee

and thy fifty. And there came down fire from Heaven, and consumed him and his fifty."

7. A second captain and his fifty men were also consumed by the fire Elijah commanded. (2 Kings 1:12)

"And Elijah answered and said to the captain of fifty, If I be a man of God, then let fire come down from Heaven, and consume thee and thy fifty. And there came down fire from Heaven, and consumed him and his fifty."

8. Elijah walked through the Jordan River on dry ground. (2 Kings 2:8)

"And Elijah took his mantle, and wrapped it together, and smote the waters, and they were divided hither and thither, so that they two went over on dry ground."

Elijah did great things by the Lord's power, and as the Lord was preparing to take him to Heaven, Elisha reached out for the treasure that was in his predecessor, seeking something that money could not buy. Something that could not be taken away from him.

Elijah advised Elisha twice to stay put and

not follow him, but Elisha would not allow anything to stop him not even the words of the prophets. He responded, *"As the LORD liveth, and as thy soul liveth, I will not leave thee."*

When you do your part, God will do His part. Elisha received a double portion of the spirit of Elijah and he performed sixteen miracles.

What's your choice today?

SIXTEEN MIRACLES OF ELISHA

1. Elisha parted the Jordan River. The last miracle that Elijah performed, became the first miracle for Elisha. (2 Kings 2:14)

"And he took the mantle of Elijah that fell from him, and smote the waters, and said, where is the lord God of Elijah? and when he also had smitten the waters, they parted hither and thither: and Elisha went over."

2. Elisha healed both the bitter water and the ground which was barren. (2 Kings 2:21-22)

"And he went forth unto the spring of the waters, and cast the salt in there, and said, Thus said the lord, I have healed these

waters; there shall not be from thence any more death or barren land. So the waters were healed unto this day according to the saying of Elisha which he spake."

3. Elisha commandeered two bears that came out of the woods and they consumed the young kids that mocked him. (2 Kings 2:24)

"And he turned back, and looked on them, and cursed them in the name of the LORD. And there came forth two she bears out of the wood, and tare forty and two children of them."

4. Elisha commanded water in the valley. (2 Kings 3:16-20)

"And he said, Thus saith the LORD, Make this valley full of ditches. For thus saith the LORD, Ye shall not see wind, neither shall ye see rain; yet that valley shall be filled with water, that ye may drink, both ye, and your cattle, and your beasts. And this is but a light thing in the sight of the LORD: he will deliver the Moabites also into your hand. And it came to pass in the morning, when the meat offering was offered, that, behold, there came water by the way of Edom, and the

country was filled with water."

5. The widow's oil was multiplied. (2 Kings4: 3-7)

"Then he said, Go, borrow thee vessels abroad of all thy neighbors, even empty vessels; borrow not a few. And when thou art come in, thou shalt shut the door upon thee and upon thy sons, and shalt pour out into all those vessels, and thou shalt set aside that which is full. So she went from him, and shut the door upon her and upon her sons, who brought the vessels to her; and she poured out. And it came to pass, when the vessels were full, that she said unto her son, Bring me yet a vessel. And he said unto her, There is not a vessel more. And the oil stayed. Then she came and told the man of God. And he said, Go, sell the oil, and pay thy debt, and live thou and thy children of the rest."

6. The barren woman of Shunem gave birth to a son. (2 Kings 4:16-17)

"And he said, About this season, according to the time of life, thou shalt embrace a son. And she said, Nay, my lord, thou man of God, do not lie unto thine handmaid. And the

woman conceived, and bare a son at that season that Elisha had said unto her, according to the time of life."

7. Elisha raised the boy from death back to life. (2 Kings 4:35-36)

"Then he returned, and walked in the house to and fro; and went up, and stretched himself upon him: and the child sneezed seven times, and the child opened his eyes. And he called Gehazi, and said, Call this Shunammite. So he called her. And when she was come in unto him, he said, Take up thy son."

8. Poisoned food was cured by Elisha. (2 Kings 4:40-41)

"So they poured out for the men to eat. And it came to pass, as they were eating of the pottage, that they cried out, and said, O thou man of God, there is death in the pot. And they could not eat thereof. But he said, Then bring meal. And he cast it into the pot; and he said, Pour out for the people, that they may eat. And there was no harm in the pot."

9. Elisha multiplied food that fed a hundred men. (2 Kings 4:43-44)

"And his servitor said, What, should I set this before an hundred men? He said again, Give the people, that they may eat: for thus saith the LORD, They shall eat, and shall leave thereof. So he set it before them, and they did eat, and left thereof, according to the word of the LORD."

10. Naaman, the Syrian, dipped himself seven times in Jordan River and was healed of leprosy, according to Elisha's instruction. (2 Kings 5:14)

"Then went he down, and dipped himself seven times in Jordan, according to the saying of the man of God: and his flesh came again like unto the flesh of a little child, and he was clean."

11. The leprosy of Naaman came upon Gehazi, according to the word of Elisha. (2 Kings 5:26-27)

"And he said unto him, Went not mine heart with thee, when the man turned again from his chariot to meet thee? Is it a time to receive money, and to receive garments, and oliveyards, and vineyards, and sheep, and oxen, and menservants, and maidservants? The leprosy therefore of Naaman shall

cleave unto thee, and unto thy seed for ever. And he went out from his presence a leper

as white as snow."

12. The axe head floated. (2 Kings 6:6-7)

"And the man of God said, Where fell it? And he showed him the place. And he cut down a stick, and cast it in thither; and the iron did swim. Therefore said he, Take it up to thee. And he put out his hand, and took it."

13. Elisha asked God to open the eyes of his servant to see the supernatural presence of God in Dothan. (2 Kings 6:17)

"And Elisha prayed, and said, LORD, I pray thee, open his eyes, that he may see. And the LORD opened the eyes of the young man; and he saw: and, behold, the mountain was full of horses and chariots of fire round about Elisha."

14. God struck Syrian soldiers with blindness, at Elisha's request. (2 Kings 6:18)

"And when they came down to him, Elisha prayed unto the LORD, and said, Smite this people, I pray thee, with blindness. And he smote them with blindness according to the

word of Elisha."

15. Elisha prophesied that the siege would be broken in twenty-four hours, and it was so. (2 Kings 7:16)

"And the people went out, and spoiled the tents of the Syrians. So a measure of fine flour was sold for a shekel, and two measures of barley for a shekel, according to the word of the LORD."

16. The second in command to the king, who doubted the prophecy of Elisha, was trampled to death, as Elisha had said that his mouth would not taste the abundance of food. (2 Kings 7:17)

"And the king appointed the lord on whose hand he leaned to have the charge of the gate: and the people trode upon him in the gate, and he died, as the man of God had said, who spake when the king came down to him."

As we have seen, Elisha received double portion of the anointing (treasure) that had been in the life of Elijah, as evidenced by the number of miracles he performed.

It was not easy for him to receive this treasure. If we go through the account of Elijah's ascension to Heaven by a chariot of fire, in 2 Kings 1, we discover that Elisha had every reason to be discouraged and refrain from following his master.

His master urged him many times to go back, but he refused. He asked him to wait at Gilgal while he went to Bethel, but he refused. At Bethel, the sons of the prophets came to distract him, but he shunned them.

His master continued, asking him to wait at Bethel while he went to Jericho, and wait at Jericho while he crossed the Jordan. In all these tests on the way, including the distractions from the sons of the prophets, Elisha refused to give up.

He had made up his mind. He had made his choice: the double portion of his master's anointing!

Child of God, make up your mind to make the right choice. Be disciplined and resilient. Your treasure will announce you!

Hallelujah!

In contrast, Gehazi, who served Elisha,

chose the wrong path. He was not seeing the treasure his master was carrying. Rather, he was looking for selfish gains. He was not interested in the anointing at all. Treasures that ***"moth and rust doth corrupt."*** (Matthew 6: 20)

When he lied, out of greed, to collect the gift Naaman brought to Elisha (which he rejected), he brought leprosy upon himself.

While Elisha chose to set his eyes on a real treasure that no man can take away, Gehazi went for momentary pleasures.

Your choice is your life!

Child of God, choose well!

CHAPTER SEVEN

3Ds FOR TREASURE

A. DREAM BIG

Dreams are one of the evidences of the spiritual realms. They provide the primary experiential truths and reality that the spiritual world controls the physical world.

This means that our dreams serve as pointers to our physical realities. This also means that your dreams play a vital role in your destiny, in the treasure you are reaching out for.

So dreams are very important in life. They motivate, inspire, improve and help you to reach out for that treasure God has deposited in you.

Praise God!

Child of God, what are your dreams?

Do you see yourself always defeated and maltreated in the dream? Do you see yourself struggling and achieving little in your dream?

The dreams that help shape your destiny are the ones that uplift and energize, that fill you with passion and make you a winner when you wake up.

They are those dreams where you see the treasure and reach out for it, grabbing it even in the midst of opposition.

Joseph, the dreamer son of Jacob in Genesis 37:5-11, is a perfect example:

"And Joseph dreamed a dream, and he told it his brethren: and they hated him yet the more. And he said unto them, Hear, I pray you, this dream which I have dreamed: For, behold, we were binding sheaves in the field, and, lo, my sheaf arose, and also stood upright; and, behold, your sheaves stood round about, and made obeisance to my sheaf. And his brethren said to him, Shalt thou indeed reign over us? Or shalt thou indeed have dominion over us? And they hated him yet the more for his dreams, and for his words. And he dreamed yet another

dream, and told it his brethren, and said, Behold, I have dreamed a dream more; and, behold, the sun and the moon and the eleven stars made obeisance to me. And he told it to his father, and to his brethren: and his father rebuked him, and said unto him, What is this dream that thou hast dreamed? Shall I and thy mother and thy brethren indeed come to bow down ourselves to thee to the earth? And his brethren envied him; but his father observed the saying."

It is one thing to dream, and another thing to DREAM BIG.

In the scripture above, Joseph dreamt big. His elder brothers hated him because his dream meant that he would rule over them. Not minding his brothers' reactions, he dreamt again, this time bigger and clearer than before.

The fact that his brothers hated him the more did not stop his dream from being fulfilled; rather, it accelerated its fulfillment.

Child of God, the presence of opposition in your life is a clear indication that the devil is afraid of you and does not want you to reach for the treasure God has prepared for you.

But, as in Joseph's life, God will take every attempt at stopping you and turn it into a stepping stone for you!

Hallelujah!

As a child of God, if you want to remain strong, you have to develop the capacity to dream big, because the God you serve is a very big God.

God is bigger than your potential; He is bigger than your credentials, your qualifications, and your financial status. He is bigger than all of your achievements or failings.

You must dream big! The scripture says in Psalm 24:1-8:

"The earth is the Lord's and the fullness thereof, the world and they that dwell therein. For He hath founded it upon the seas and established it upon the floods. Who shall ascend the hills of the Lord? He that has a Clean heart and clean hands…Lift up your heads, oh ye gates, be ye lifted up ye everlasting doors, that the King of Glory shall come in. Who is this King of Glory? The Lord strong and Mighty! The Lord mighty in battle…"

It is an error for you to wake up in the morning and wish for the earth to give you what it has in store for you.

Big error!

Life is not "*Que cera, cera*, whatever will be, will be." That is not how things work. You have to understand that the earth can only produce what you have planted in it. So when you wake up in the morning, plant your seed for the day. Declare what you want from the day.

Every day as you wake, you have to declare positive, Spirit-filled words to carry you through the day.

I challenge you to do this every day, and you will see how your life will be transformed.

Praise God!

As I said earlier, **YOU MUST DREAM BIG because you are serving a BIG GOD.**

Dreaming big makes you stronger. It increases your expectation and faith. It enables you to experience the power of God that makes all things possible.

David declared this in Psalms 18:29:

"For by thee I have run through a troop; and by my God have I leaped over a wall."

Big dream equals great expectation. The passage above expresses the words of a man who had seen the victory even before the battle. David was living in the reality of the bigness of his God. No wonder he never lost a battle!

Child of God, I pray that God will increase your capacity to dream big and you will reach out for the best He has for you, in Jesus' mighty name!

B. DISCOVER YOURSELF

Child of God, you need to discover yourself.

So many believers are moving about casually without knowing what God has put in them. You must discover yourself to know and see all the treasures that God has embedded in you.

You need to discover the gifts, the talents, the virtues, etc. that God has deposited in you. You need to discover yourself, to know what the anointing of God can do in your life. You need to discover what it means to be a son of God or a daughter of Zion. You need to discover what it means to be a partaker of the divine nature of God.

In Psalm 139:14, David made a declaration out of self discovery:

"I will praise thee; for I am fearfully and wonderfully made: marvelous are thy works; and that my soul knoweth right well."

By this assertion, David does not need anybody to validate or approve his personality. He does not need anyone to tell him who he is. He discovered himself and he lived as the man after God's heart.

Child of God, the day you discover yourself marks a turning point in your life. May that day be today!

How do you discover yourself? Go to the Lord your Creator. Seek an encounter with your Maker!

No one can know all the functions of an electronic gadget better than the manufacturer. That is why the manufacturer provides a manual, so that you can study and know what the gadget can or cannot do.

A lot of people have lost the manual of their lives through sin and ignorance. For some people, their manual was stolen by the devil.

By the mercy of God, today you shall discover and recover all!

Hallelujah!

When Abram encountered God, he became Abraham the father of many nations. Jacob encountered Him and became Israel, a prince that has prevailed with God and man. Moses became the deliverer of Israel from Egypt. Gideon became the mighty man of valor that defeated the Midianites. And today, as you encounter Him, may you see and manifest the great destiny He has ordained for you!

Hallelujah!

If you do not discover yourself, you will become irrelevant. Lack of self-discovery can result in loss of confidence, low self-esteem and other negative feelings.

You have to discover yourself to know how great God has created you to be. You have to discover yourself to know that unique quality which God has put in you. That is the rare quality that distinguishes you from other people.

Beloved, know that God has made you special. You are not an ordinary person, because God's power in you transcends what a layman would refer to as ordinary in nature. The power of God in you transcends every form of disability and limitation.

By the special grace of God, on five different occasions God has raised dead people in my ministry. However, some time ago, there were two physically challenged people I was praying for God to heal. One was in a wheel chair and the other was dumb. I had been praying for them for a while and God had not healed them. I was asking God for answers, as well as reminding Him of the miracles of raising the dead. I was seriously seeking answers from God concerning these people.

Finally, the Lord spoke to me. He said, "I don't see things the way you see them." The Lord went on to tell me that all His children are beautiful. He said that none of His children is disabled or handicapped, and that He sees all His children exactly the way He made them, and not as we mortals see them.

God continued to tell me that all His children are perfect, and that, if only they would look beyond their physical disabilities and discover themselves, then they would do great exploits in spite of their disabilities.

This reminds me of one man I read about some time ago. He does not have arms like you and I. it is, however, so surprising to see that this man is working as an Engine Designer in an Auto-Engineering outfit. He draws and designs with his toes. He works with a computer and carries out his duties with so much precision that he is one of the highest paid in his company.

This guy just discovered himself! What are you waiting for? Child of God, you need to discover yourself!

C. DWELL IN HIS PRESENCE

Beloved, the best place to be is where God is. You need to dwell in God's presence in prayer, studying the Word, and in fellowship.

The presence of God is like an incubator that nurtures and hatches out the treasure in you. It is like the blacksmith's fire that refines crude matter until it becomes pure.

The presence of God prunes, bends, heals, refines, revives, renews, refreshes and rebrands talents, gifts and treasures for Kingdom assignment to the glory of God.

Child of God, for you to reach out for that treasure, you need to dwell in His presence!

One of the things that happens to you when you dwell in God's presence is that His glory will rub-off on you. Like someone that visited a perfume factory, the aroma of the perfume will settle on your clothes. When you make a fire with wood, the smell of the smoke from the wood as you fan the flame will be unmistakably on you.

That is what happens when you dwell in God's presence. YOU SMELL LIKE GOD! Hallelujah!

The presence of God transforms the raw gift and treasures in you to usable virtues and abilities. The more you stay in His presence, the more you will be like HIM.

In the book of 2 Corinthians, it says:

"But we all, with open face beholding as in a

glass the glory of the Lord, are changed into the same image from glory to glory, even as by the Spirit of God." (3:18)

Moses stayed with God for forty days on Mount Sinai, and when he came down, his face shone. People could not look at him anymore, because the glory of God that had rubbed off on him was radiating.

With that, Moses led the Israelites with ease. The treasure in him had been refined. Praise God!

In the same way, Joshua the son of Nun, who took over the mantle of leadership from Moses, discovered himself in the presence of God. In the book of Exodus, the Bible records that:

"And the Lord spake to unto Moses face to face, as a man speaketh unto his friend. And turned again into the camp, but his servant Joshua the son of Nun, a young man departed not out of the tabernacle." (33:11)

The presence of God is the breeding ground of gifts, and the harnessing place for treasures.

Despite the seventy elders and leaders

anointed to assist Moses, as may be seen in Numbers 11:16-30, God chose Joshua to lead the people because he was a man addicted to His presence.

The leader in Joshua was made in God's presence. The treasure in him was pruned and harnessed in God's presence. May nothing take you away from His presence!

In Act 4:13, the Bible says that:

"Now when they saw the boldness of Peter and John that they were unlearned men, they marveled: and they took knowledge of them, that they had been with Jesus."

In the scripture, Peter and John were ordinary, illiterate men, known by all the people. But when they began to preach the gospel, after Jesus had risen and ascended, the people observed that they had become bold and spoke wisdom and mysteries that their teachers of the law (Pharisees and Sadducees) did not know.

They quickly remarked that THEY HAD BEEN WITH JESUS.

What happened there was that the treasure in them (Peter and John) opened up, because they spent time with Jesus.

Child of God, where do you spend your time? You, who God has called into the ministry, how long do you spend in His presence, reading the Bible and/or praying?

I urge you today to dwell in His presence like never before, and get ready to experience a deeper manifestation of His power and glory in your life and ministry!

CHAPTER EIGHT

DUTY CALL

For what reason has the Lord made you?

Why has God taken so much time and energy to form you and deposit treasures (gift and talents) in you?

For what purpose did God give His only begotten Son to die for you? What is the purpose of your salvation? Why is the treasure in you?

In the book of Exodus the Bible record thus:

"And the LORD spake unto Moses, Go unto Pharaoh, and say unto him, Thus saith the LORD, Let My people go, that they may serve Me." (8:1)

The Lord told Moses that He wanted His people Israel to leave Egypt for one purpose, and that was to serve Him.

All the miracles and plagues that were seen in Egypt were just for His purpose to be accomplished: "*...that they may serve Me*"

This is very instructive. **God saved you so you can serve Him**. He delivered Israel from the Egyptians and all the nations that rose against them in the wilderness until He brought them to the Promised Land for this very purpose. God repeated this instruction to Moses to tell Pharaoh, in chapter 9, verse 1. This is the heartbeat of God. This is why He created man. This is why He redeemed man. JUST TO SERVE HIM!

And in the New Testament, the Holy Spirit made it even clearer. In Ephesians 4:11-12, the fivefold ministry offices are revealed as the means of preparing men to serve Him:

"And he gave some, apostles; and some, prophets; and some, evangelists; and some, pastors and teachers; for the perfecting of the saints, for the work of the ministry, for the edifying of the body of Christ:"

Child of God, you have been forgiven, and sanctified and endowed to serve the Lord. God has deposited treasures in you so you can use them to serve Him. Whatever type of gift you have, it is for the perfecting of the saints, for the work of the ministry and for the edification of the Church.

So with the treasure God has deposited in you, you can serve in different capacities as we will see below:

TREASURE IN YOU MAKES YOU A MINISTER.

As stated in the previous chapter, what God has deposited in you makes you a minister. This is so because the treasure in you consists of the supernatural power of God.

What an incentive!

In other words, you are no longer an ordinary person. From the moment you realize this truth, you will cease to be that struggling, inactive, complaining and depressed person that you used to be. You will no longer be that person that gets angry at the slightest provocation or that is always defeated and frustrated.

Rather, you will become a victor, a success and a winner - a solution to the problems of people around you! You will bring hope, peace, healing, miracles, signs and wonders by the power of God at work in you.

Praise God!

IT HELPS YOU TO SERVE

The treasure that God has deposited in you positions you to serve because someone needs the treasure that is in you. Your church needs what is in you.

Sometimes, when you quarrel with your spouse, you want to drag it to more than a day or two. What you do not know is that everyone needs someone to talk to. Even in the midst of the quarrel, you need someone to talk to. Spouses should serve one another. No one is a utility tool.

You need to understand that the power of God in you helps you to serve others.

IT HELPS YOU TO TRANSFORM LIVES

Beloved, the treasure in you propels you to transform lives. Because of what God has put in you, you will see lives transformed, you will see lives changed, and watch sinners turn to saints.

Praise God!

God's treasure in you gives you the opportunity to see ordinary people transformed to very important people. That is why you are an important personality. The Church of God needs you; your nation needs you; you are needed everywhere.

Do you know why you are needed for that job? It is because of that unique treasure in you that brings about a transformation. When you discover that there is gold in a particular piece of land, you hurry to buy it. When you remember your paycheck as a worker, you go to work. And if you know that Jesus Christ will save you, you give your life to Him without delay.

In chapter two, I told to you that the parable of the talents is an excellent illustration revealing that God wants His children to use the gifts He has implanted in us for His glory and for the expansion of the Kingdom of Heaven into the lives of men. That is the increase He seeks.

Let me further say that many professing Christians have been wonderfully taught in the truths of the Word of God, and thereby, are filled with understanding and wisdom. As you read this, you might be one of those who are filled with treasures from the Word of God – ALL of which are tremendous treasures He has entrusted to you – but, could it be that you are one who sits back doing nothing with these great treasures? Are you burying God's treasures?

Beloved, I urge you: Do not hold back. Souls are waiting to find the treasure that you have received.

Let His loving compassion fill you so that you greatly desire to freely give as you have freely received.

There is something in you that transforms lives. Praise God!

IT HELPS YOU TO OVERCOME YOUR TRIALS

One of the incentives you receive is the ability to overcome all trials.

Hallelujah!

Do you know why? It is because what you are going through is worth your while so far as it results in glory to God.

For instance, you are not being a good husband or wife because you want to please your spouse. No, not at all! You are being a good spouse because you want to please God. It gives God glory.

You are giving in the church because you know that the glory goes to God. You are serving in the choir because God takes the glory. And whatsoever you are required to do in the choir, you patiently go through it because His glory is an incentive.

Despite what you experience among the members, the pastors or anyone, you will bear it because the glory goes to God. If you have the understanding that it is God who takes all the glory for what you are doing, believe me, you will overcome.

Problems arise when you think that what you are doing is for people. And that is when you say that Mr. A or Mrs. B is ungrateful.

However, when you know your labor is for God's pleasure, then you do not need anybody to tell you that he/she is grateful to you.

Sometimes, we find ourselves expecting

people to say "Thank you" to us. Let me give you this Kingdom secret: if you do things without expecting a "Thank you" from people, God will thank you. Even when people deliberately refuse to thank you when you do good to them, Heaven will thank you.

IT HELPS YOU TO LIVE AND MAINTAIN KINGDOM LIFESTYLE

You are not coming to God to see what to take or grab. Rather, you are coming to see if there is an opportunity for you to exhibit what is in you.

Every day you find yourself praying for the universe to provide you with opportunities to serve. As a result, you jump into any available opportunity you see, not because you are the only one available for the role, but because you are jumping into (securing) your future.

You are not a liability in the Kingdom. You have something in you. As a matter of fact, everyone has something to offer. You cannot afford to be a liability anywhere at all because of the treasure in you.

All you have to do is to reach out for the

treasure and if you do, you will find out that the excellency of power will be of God alone.

You need to know that any time you take a step of faith, God always steps in. He sits back and says that He is the one who put the treasure in you and He will perfect it and take you to the next level.

CONCLUSION

God Almighty created man in His own image. You are God's own superscription.

When man got lost, God did everything to reconcile man to Himself. God emptied Heaven on man's behalf by allowing His only begotten Son to die on the cross for man's redemption.

Oh, how God treasures man! What is man that God is mindful of him?

It is time for you to dream big, discover yourself and dwell where God Is. If you need something from me, you have to come to me. In the same way, if you want God to draw near to you, you must draw near to Him, then He will draw near to you.

Do not be fooled by the deceitfulness of this world. Reach out for treasures, things of great value; go for things with eternal value and unleash everything that God has deposited in you to serve others.

In conclusion, I want to leave you with this amazing scripture by Apostle Paul, in the book of 1 Corinthians:

"But as it is written, Eye hath not seen, nor ears heard, neither have entered into the heart of man, the things which God hath prepared for them that love him." (2:9)

Have you ever wondered why God hides what He wants to do for us?

He does so because, if He let us see what He wants us to be, we would not do anything other than sit down and cross our legs.

Knowing when our lifting will come could make some people stop going to church, stop praying, stop reading the Bible and, instead, begin counting the days.

It is only revealed through the Holy Spirit. And when you receive this revelation, you will get busy and start the work of God as you wait for that day to come.

There is always an appointed time, and when that time comes, the promise of God will come to pass in your life.

www.ingramcontent.com/pod-product-compliance
Lightning Source LLC
Chambersburg PA
CBHW071147090426
42736CB00012B/2256